COCO CHANEL

T&J

Published by TAJ Books International LLC 2014
5501 Kincross Lane
Charlotte, North Carolina, USA
28277

www.tajbooks.com
www.tajminibooks.com

All notations of errors or omissions (author inquiries, permissions) concerning the
content of this book should be addressed to
info@tajbooks.com.

ISBN 978-1-84406-339-0

978-1-62732-017-7 Paperback

Printed in China

1 2 3 4 5 18 17 16 15 14

COCO CHANEL

T&J

ISABELLA ALSTON & KATHRYN DIXON

COCO CHANEL: HER LIFE

Coco Chanel is undoubtedly one of the most famous fashion designers of all time. In testament to this, she was named by *Time* magazine as one of the 100 most influential people of the 20th century. Her life was filled with romance, intrigue, and scandal. Her business acumen and groundbreaking talent took her far beyond her humble beginnings. Her designs broke numerous barriers, and her influence on style and aesthetic forever changed the world, especially for women.

Chanel understood how to get what she wanted from life and never hesitated to pursue her grand vision. In many ways she was responsible for a major first step toward women's liberation, doing so through the world of fashion by freeing women from the strictures of corsets and adapting menswear, specifically pants, to the female body. In addition to her brilliant new style, Chanel introduced her own brand of perfume, N°5. It was the first scent associated with a designer. Today most fashion houses have their own fragrance line, but it was Chanel who started the trend.

Gabrielle Bonheur Chanel was born August 19, 1883, in a poorhouse in Saumur, France. The nuns who ran the poorhouse were kind to Chanel's unwed mother, Eugénie Jeanne Devolle (known as Jeanne), a laundress, leading her to name her newborn daughter after one of the sisters, Gabrielle Bonheur. Chanel's father, Henri-Albert Chanel (known as Albert), was an itinerant salesman who was traveling at the time of his daughter's birth. In many ways it was appropriate for Chanel to be brought into the world by nuns, since she would soon find herself in their care.

A number of years later, Chanel would attempt to have her birth records erased out of a burning, undying desire to hide her humble upbringing, although she was unsuccessful in doing so. Interestingly, a clerical error on her birth certificate misspelled her name as "Chasnel" making it slightly easier for her to conceal the truth about her past. Her mother's first child, Julia, was also born out of wedlock. Jeanne's peasant family was unable to support her and pressured Albert to marry

Gabrielle Chanel, 1909

her when Chanel was a bit over a year old. The couple had four more children, each born two years apart: Alphonse, Antoinette, Lucien, and Augustin. The last, Augustin, died in infancy.

The poverty-stricken Chanel family lived in the small railway town of Brive-la-Gaillarde in central southwest France between Paris and Toulouse. Very little about Chanel's early childhood is known with any veracity, most details being fabricated from Chanel's desire for a socially acceptable background. What can be derived from the stories Chanel told is that she felt unloved by her father, who likely resented his children and wife for forcing him into a life he had previously been able to successfully avoid.

In 1895, when Chanel was 11 years old, her 31-year-old mother became gravely ill while her father was away on a sales trip. The children were found in their mother's wintry cold bedroom by their father upon his return, her mother's lifeless body—ravaged by poverty, pregnancy, and respiratory illness—stiff on the bed. How long the girls were in the room with their dead mother is unknown, though the trauma of the situation must have been excruciating for all. But before the ink

At the seaside resort of Deauville in northern France standing in front of her shop, aptly named Gabrielle Chanel, with her aunt Adrienne, 1913 (above); another view from Deauville (right)

6

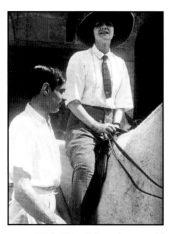

With "Boy" Capel, an avid horseman, in 1918, a year before he was killed in a car accident (above); a caricature of Capel and Chanel dancing drawn by the caricaturist Georges Goursat (1863–1934), known as Sem, in 1913 (top right); and Capel and Chanel in a relaxed moment (bottom right)

Mademoiselle Chanel (second from right) with Arthur "Boy" Capel (far right) and others in front of her Deauville shop

had dried on Jeanne's death certificate, her husband was busy ridding himself of the children. The boys were dropped off with a peasant family who most certainly paid a small fee for the additional hands to help keep the household running. Chanel, along with her sisters, Julia and Antoinette, were brought to a Cistercian-run orphanage in nearby Aubazine.

Just as Chanel made up stories about her early childhood, she also created a life for herself during the period she stayed with the nuns. She told her friends and interviewers alike that after her mother's death her father took the children to family members who reared them. Regardless of how she described those years in her life, one very real outcome was that she learned to sew, a skill taught to her by the nuns. Another outcome was that she, by all accounts, emerged stridently anti-Semitic. This trait, along with her cozy relationships with German officers and German sympathizers, fed suspicions during the World War II years that she was a Nazi spy. The very pragmatic Chanel, however, may only have been protecting her livelihood, albeit at the cost of appearing disloyal and unpatriotic to her homeland.

During the seven years that Chanel lived with the nuns, her father never visited her, essentially abandoning her along with her sisters. But as an adult, Chanel claimed that her father stayed in touch with her and even sent gifts, likely as an effort to hide the pain of being tossed aside without either parent for comfort. According to Hamish Bowles writing in *Vogue* in 2005, the medieval convent experience was so seared into Chanel's consciousness that it impacted her design aesthetic through product packaging that mirrored the stark white convent walls with their dark black trim and through the elegant interlocking Cs of the Chanel logo inspired by the abbey's stained-glass windows. The five-star pattern on the convent's stone mosaic floors influenced many of Chanel's jewelry designs, and her intricately beaded and embellished evening dresses are redolent of the mosaic patterning so prolific at the Aubazine abbey.

*The flagship Chanel boutique
at 31 rue Cambon in Paris*

During her teenage years, she discovered a love of romantic novels, such as *Wuthering Heights* by Emily Brontë. Perhaps not just an escape from reality, these romances may have also fueled the creative re-telling of her personal history to make it (and her) more appealing than would otherwise have been the case. Nevertheless, her behavior in later years indicates that she may have truly liked life at the abbey. With the nuns and their charges living a frugal and contemplative life, Chanel had ample time to daydream, read, plan, and perfect talents, such as sewing. She continued to return to the abbey even after she had become a world famous designer. Those who lived near the abbey recalled for years seeing her chauffeured black car pull up to the abbey where she would spend the day visiting the nuns and walking the halls she knew as a young girl. She always departed before nightfall, leaving the sisters with financial donations to support their work.

The relationship Chanel had with her older sister, Julia, is basically unknown. As Chanel told it, Julia died when she slit her wrists after discovering that her husband had a mistress. At her death, Chanel assumed Julia's six-year-old son's care. His name was André Palasse. André never lived with Chanel. She sent him to an English boarding school. Some suspected that André may in fact have been Chanel's child. No proof has ever surfaced to support that contention.

In 1901, when Chanel turned 18 years old, she entered the Notre Dame School in Moulins as a charity pupil. The abbey prohibited girls over 18 to remain there unless they had chosen to follow the "religious path" and join the order. This future was certainly not in the stars for Chanel, who was in many ways the exact opposite of piety and humbleness. Chanel did eventually establish a relationship with her paternal grandparents and grew quite close to her aunt, Adrienne, probably because the two were very near the same age. It was a bittersweet time in Chanel's life because most of the other students at the school were from relatively affluent families and shunned her. To find solace she delved deeper into her love of reading and sewing, which ultimately paid off quite handsomely in the end.

In 1920, after "Boy" Capell's death, with newly cropped hair

Soon after her arrival at the Notre Dame School, Chanel and Adrienne found jobs as assistants to a seamstress in Moulins. They shared a small attic room located above the seamstress' shop and earned extra pay working weekends for a nearby tailor. The men who frequented the tailor were quite taken with the pair of young girls and began to court them, escorting them to shows at La Rotonde, a local outdoor concert hall. Both girls soon were determined to become cabaret stars, especially Chanel, who quickly gained a regular spot in the program.

During this interlude in her life Chanel earned her famous nickname, Coco. Two songs compete for the honor of naming her. One is "Qui qu'a vu Coco?" ("Who has seen Coco?"), a song about a girl who lost her dog. The other is "Ko Ko Rik Ko" (the French equivalent of "Cock-a-doodle-doo"). Because these two songs were the extent of her repertoire, both can lay claim to her alliterative appellation.

Étienne Balsan, a scion of a well-to-do family of textile industrialists soon took Chanel as his mistress. Balsan's family had made their fortune by providing the French army with blue wool for their uniforms. About the time that Balsan and Chanel met, he resigned his commission as a cavalry officer to pursue his true love of horses and polo. The two new lovers resided at Balsan's chateau, Royallieu, near the town of Compiegne where Chanel eagerly adopted the pastimes of the aristocratic class—hunting and riding. Interestingly, the chateau was an old abbey; once again Chanel found respite under a godly roof.

Balsan's secluded chateau provided a much needed physical and psychological retreat for the young woman who had struggled with poverty and abandonment most of her short life. The three years that Chanel lived with Balsan at Royallieu are just as obscure as the rest of her youth. Forever loyal, Balsan always refused to disclose any information about Chanel when reporters or biographers inquired about his relationship with her. In many ways, Chanel owed her great success and fame to Balsan, for he and his connections accelerated her escape from a drab life in Moulins. Given Chanel's aspirations, however, it is likely that eventually she would have found another

1920

sponsor with the financial means to improve her position. Even after the pair split romantically, they remained close as friends, and Balsan's death in 1953 hit Chanel hard.

At the time Chanel moved into Royallieu, the dancer Émilienne d'Alençon, with whom Balsan was involved, was still living there as his mistress. According to some, Chanel at first was made to eat her meals with the servants. Eventually, d'Alençon took another lover and departed, which finally allowed Chanel free run of the estate. Chanel despised the clothes that d'Alençon wore, ridiculing them as "heavy gowns and spotted veils," and prided herself on her more modern, unencumbered style. Spending much time in the company of horses, she found wearing tailor-made equestrian clothing made her life easier and facilitated her active lifestyle. This fondness for menswear-like pants would be reflected in her early clothing designs and mark her style as liberating for women.

Chanel's recollection of the time she spent at Royallieu was of extreme homesickness for the life she left at the abbey. It was also the origin of her notorious ability to fabricate her past. Given the importance placed at that time on rank and social status, it is not surprising that she liberally embellished the story of her upbringing. Alone in a foreign environment, oppressed and generally dismissed, Chanel's need to create a more glamorous past was certainly self-preservation at work. Balsan's friends tried to persuade him to send her back to Moulins, asserting she was too young for the role of mistress. Chanel had lied about her age, telling Balsan she was several years older than she was. Dismissed by those to the manor bred, she found solace in the company of the courtesans–even d'Alençon–who frequented the chateau for the parties that Balsan regularly threw. It was at one of these glamorous gatherings that Chanel met her next love, Arthur "Boy" Capel.

Capel, a Brit, came to France amidst a swirl of romantic intrigue about his background. Rumors variably linked him to the British aristocracy or identified him as the illegitimate son of a wealthy French businessman. Irrespective of his bloodlines, he was quite the playboy as well as a prolific polo player,

Chanel and the Grand Duke Dmitri Pavlovich, one of the few Romanovs to escape murder by the Bolsheviks after the Russian Revolution, c. 1921. Pavlovich's diaries record relationships with many fascinating women of his day, but the affair he is most remembered for was with Coco Chanel, whom he met in Paris. Their relationship lasted about three years, beginning in spring 1921.

Modeling her jersey designs in 1929; note that Chanel has paired the same loose striped, sleeveless top, long, multi-stranded pearls, and strapped two-tone shoes with different suits

Chanel at the races with her lover, the Duke of Westminster, the richest man in England at the time, 1924

19

1928

probably why he and Balsan were such close acquaintances. According to Chanel, she met Capel when she and Balsan were in Pau, a small French town in the Pyrenees. She was immediately taken by Capel, falling in love with the handsome, very tanned, and attractive man. Although she claims never to have spoken to Capel during their mutual visit to Pau, she jumped on the train with him as he returned to Paris. Chanel claimed that Balsan threw a fit over her departing Pau with Capel, yet she left anyway, realizing that all it took was jealousy for Balsan to admit his true feelings for her.

Capel and Chanel had a lengthy romance, yet not always a happy one. Capel was never truly faithful to Chanel, but the pendulum swung both ways as Chanel continued her dalliances with Balsan. By this point, Chanel was already experimenting with making her own hats, the simplicity of which proved to be instantly popular with d'Alençon and other well-known *cocottes* (courtesans) of Paris. These first clients wore her designs on stage and around town, with magazines describing their stunning new hats in detail, quite effectively advertising Chanel's creations.

Although she was a "kept woman" living in a suit at the Ritz in Paris paid for by Capel, she

With Vera Bate, 1928

1929

was restive, unhappy to rely on a man for her living expenses. She negotiated with both Balsan and Capel regarding backing her in a millinery business, which she viewed as a way to make her own living. The two men agreed to share the expenses for launching her business venture. Balsan provided her with an apartment and shop space in Paris at 160 Boulevard Malesherbes. Capel provided the funds. Chanel's hats were uniquely modern and chic, free of the excessive decoration and frills that adorned the hats worn by ladies of the Belle Époque era. Chanel initially purchased straw boaters from a department store and trimmed them with ribbon. So simple. It wasn't long before some of the most influential Parisian women were flocking to her store to purchase Chanel's avantgarde designs.

Encouraged by her success, in 1910 she procured even more funds from her financial backers and lovers to open a millinery shop at 21 rue Cambon in Paris. Chanel was blessed with an astute mind for business and within a couple of years broadened her product line to include clothes, the designs of which were influenced by her girlish figure,

Photo by Man Ray, 1930

Pants, pants, and more pants! Chanel expanded women's fashion boundaries into the realm of men's fashion to capture the comfort and freedom for women that only men had previously enjoyed. From left to right, Chanel wears pants paired with a striped sailor top at her Villa La Pausa in southern France; with her signature pearls on the Lido in Venice accompanied by Duke Larino of Rome; and with narrow belt, collier, and hat while she enjoys a relaxing respite (1920s and early 1930s).

love of sports and the outdoors, and her taste for simplicity. Her first prêt-à-porter shop opened in the resort town of Deauville in 1913 from which she offered casual wear for women.

Limited by her Paris lease to the sale of hats only, in 1919 she moved a few doors down the street to 31 rue Cambon, where the flagship Chanel store is still located today. As a means of advertising her boutique, Chanel adorned her sister Antoinette and dear friend and aunt, Adrienne, with her clothes and they strode the streets of Paris. Potential customers were as curious about the new designer as the new designs. The story goes that a woman admitted openly to Chanel that she had come to the store purely to see her, the eccentric creature behind the latest Parisian fashion trends.

Out on the town...in pants

Chanel struggled daily with anxiety attacks. She suffered from fainting spells and a mild form of agoraphobia or claustrophobia, so much so that she stopped going to mass. The anxiety that plagued her was likely a combination of past trauma and uncertainty about the future, especially her relationship with Capel. But her work gave her a sense of stability that always tended to right her ship. She would eventually discover that Capel had deposited bank securities to guarantee her business, meaning that what she was earning was not paying off her debt

Wearing her new lounging pajamas, 1931

to him as she had been led to believe. This realization was the last straw for Chanel, who from that point on vowed to make a fortune and secure her financial independence once and for all. Chanel asserted later that Capel told her he had funded her business to give her a plaything, but alas it gave her freedom.

At the outbreak of World War I, Chanel's business was flourishing. Capel, having joined the British army, urged Chanel to leave Paris for Deauville, the small seaside resort in the north of France where she had opened a boutique. Capel rented a villa there, allegedly for his ponies, but it also afforded Chanel a place to live. Deauville was the perfect spot for Chanel to find success. The majority of the town's inhabitants were wealthy, elite members of Parisian society escaping the confines of the city, the perfect target market for Chanel's designs. Furthermore, the relaxed, yet simultaneously chic, style that epitomized her clothing was infinitely more suited to the resort lifestyle than the heavier fabrics and excessive material that dominated Belle Époque fashions.

In Monte Carlo, 1931, with the dancer Serge Lifar of the Ballet Russes

Chanel (right) with the actress Ina Claire on the set of the movie The Greeks Had a Word for Them *for which Chanel designed the costumes, 1931*

Inevitable wartime restrictions made traditional fabrics very hard to come by. For many dressmakers this presented an insurmountable problem, but not for Chanel. Her business acuity and knack for making the ordinary extraordinary allowed her to see the possibilities of a fabric once only used for men's underwear—jersey. Jersey was a natural for Chanel who used its fluidity to flatter the female form and to give casual clothes needed comfort and give. Thanks to her continued success, even in the midst of a devastating world war, Chanel opened a third shop in 1915 in Biarritz, a luxurious resort town in southwestern France on the Bay of Biscay.

Biarritz's reputation as the "in" spot was cemented when in the mid-19th century the wife of Napoleon III, Empress Eugénie, built a vacation palace there. Fifty years later a casino was added to the mix of pleasures the town offers visitors. To this day, Biarritz still attracts the rich and famous, but no longer boasts a Chanel boutique; it was closed in 1939 along with the Deauville boutique at the start of World War II. The vacationers in Biarritz, just as in Deauville, snatched up Chanel's jersey jackets, skirts, and striped boat-neck shirts, reminiscent of those sailors wore. In the throes of war, the simplicity of Chanel's fashions became increasingly appropriate.

Hoisted on the shoulders of the dancer Serge Lifar, Chanel is draped in the pearls bestowed upon her regularly by her lover, the Duke of Westminster; trimmed in her jewelried cuffs designed by Fulco Santostefano della Cerda, the Duke of Verdura, who was in her employ; and cork sandals made by a Venice bootmaker at her behest (above)

Wearing one of the earliest Chanel suits, 1932 (right)

Capel may truly have loved Chanel, but he did not view her as marriage material. He married the British socialite, Diana Wyndham, the daughter of a lord, in 1918. His engagement and marriage did not deter him from his affair with Chanel, but her dreams of one day marrying him were permanently crushed. In December 1919 Capel was killed in a car accident. The loss devastated Chanel. He had been traveling from Paris to Cannes with his mechanic when one of the car's tires exploded and he lost control of the car, injuring the mechanic and killing Capel.

Chanel heard the news a few days after the accident from her old friend, Leon de Laborde, whom she had met at Royallieu years earlier. Chanel quickly packed a bag and drove with Laborde to Cannes where Capel's funeral was to be held. Chanel sat up the entire night, refusing the bed that Capel's sister offered her, never shedding a tear. The next day, rather than attend the funeral, she went to the scene of the accident. The charred skeleton of the car had not yet been removed from the road and the wreckage was there for the shattered Chanel to relive Capel's last moments; his body had been burned beyond recognition. Her emotions finally overwhelmed her as she collapsed to the ground and wept. Capel was completely lost to her in an emotional and physical sense, yet his soul remained tethered to her through the business he had helped her establish.

In testament to how much Chanel meant to him, Capel left her £40,000 from his estate, not that much less than the £70,000 he left his wife. A bit of a comeuppance to Chanel, however, was that he left an equal amount to an Italian countess, presumably another of his lovers, whose husband had been killed during the war. As was typical of Chanel, she used the money wisely and invested in her growing fashion house by expanding her Paris shop. This is perhaps the exact purpose that Capel had in mind for her inheritance.

With Fulco di Verdura at the Bal des Valses hosted by Baron Nicolas "Niki" de Gunzburg and Prince and Princess Jean-Louis de Faucigny-Lucinge in July 1934; the theme of the evening was the Imperial Court of Vienna, Austria, in 1860.

Chanel had enough money left over to buy a villa in Garches, a largely residential community on the western outskirts of Paris. She named the villa Bel Respiro, or "deep breath" in Italian, precisely what Chanel hoped her secluded villa would allow her to take. In mourning for her beloved Capel, she ordered that all the window shades be painted black so that when they were closed the house would look as if it had shut its eyes. In a sweeping gesture of mourning, she had turned her previous bedroom black, from the walls to the bed linens, following Capel's death. The paint was hardly dry when she regretted the decision.

By this time, Chanel was setting style, not merely adding to the conversation. The fashion magazine *Vogue* featured her sports suits in 1916, the year her first couture collection debuted. Her contribution was not just in clothing and millinery, but in her personal style as well, and could be no more cutting edge than when she sheared off her long, thick hair. The public adored her new schoolboy bob and it rapidly became the rage along with the red-hot jazz of roaring-twenties Paris. True or false, Chanel's tale of how she came to cut her hair just adds to her allure as a mysterious muse in the world of fashion. She claimed that an explosion of a gas burner in her apartment resulted not only in her radical haircut, but also inspired her "little black dress" that quickly became a classic wardrobe staple for women of all ages, then and now. As she was dressing for an evening at the opera, she found she could not get the water warm enough to wash her face. She was dressed in a simply cut white dress. As she tried to adjust the pilot light, suddenly it exploded and covered her once-pristine dress with soot, turning it black. Her hair was also singed, so she grabbed a nearby pair of scissors and lopped it off into a bob. After Boy Capel died so suddenly and harshly, Chanel's "little black dress" probably took on new meaning for her as yet another symbol of mourning for her lost lover.

The next object of Chanel's affections was not a man, but a woman. The exact nature of the relationship was never known, perhaps more a love built on mutual admiration and infatuation, although the gossips speculate that it was in fact a romantic love. The woman who

A portrait by Man Ray, c. 1935

Chanel doted on was Misia Sert, one of the most well-known women in Paris at the time.

Misia was born in St. Petersburg in 1872. Her father was a sculptor, Cyprian Godebski, who was originally from Poland. Misia's mother, Sophie, the daughter of the virtuoso Belgian cellist Adrien-François Servais, died giving birth to her, setting off a series of events uncannily similar to Chanel's own childhood. Godebski had no real interest in his child, sending her to a convent in the heart of Paris at the age of 10. She only occasionally visited her father and stepmother in their mansion in Paris' Polish district. When Misia was 15 years old her stepmother died and she was made to kiss her corpse just as Chanel claims she was made to kiss her mother's corpse.

Like Chanel, Misia tried to alter her birth certificate. But unlike Chanel, Misia's life stories, despite often sounding too fantastic to be true, are all verifiably accurate. Misia married a Polish lawyer when she was 21 years old, divorcing four years later. She then engaged in a series of fast and furious romances, eventually marrying Alfred Edwards, a wealthy newspaper magnate. Edwards proved to be exceptionally jealous. Misia recounted how, during a trip to Madrid, Spain, he locked her in the hotel room all day long.

Eventually, Edwards lost interest in Misia, shifting his affections to a bisexual prostitute-turned-actress, Genevieve Lantelme, whom he married a year after his and Misia's divorce was finalized. Lantelme died two years later from falling off–or being pushed, it was never clear–Edwards' yacht into the Seine. Three years later, Edwards was dead. In the meantime, Misia met José-Maria Sert. Sert was a prominent artist. His frescoes and Rococo-esque murals adorn the ballroom at the Waldorf Astoria in New York City as well as the walls of Rockefeller Center. The couple quickly became very prominent in the Paris social scene although they did not marry until 1920, a dozen years after their first introduction.

Chanel and Misia met in 1917 at a dinner party hosted by a mutual acquaintance, Cecile Sorel. Sorel, a glamorous French stage actress, was a frequent client of Chanel. Misia, enthralled

Framed by her coromandel screens in a photograph by Boris Lipnitzki, 1937

by Chanel's quiet, mysterious aura across the dining table, requested that she be seated beside her after the meal. They exchanged pleasantries until Chanel rose to leave. Misia complimented her on her red velvet, fur-trimmed evening coat. Chanel promptly draped it over Misia's shoulders, insisting it was now hers. Misia refused the generous gift, but Chanel's gesture bewitched her.

The next morning Misia unexpectedly dropped by Chanel's boutique, and Chanel invited Misia and José to dinner at her apartment that evening. It was the beginning of a very close friendship, so close that Chanel felt throughout her life that Misia was her only true female friend. Even so, she came to believe that Misia's strong attachment to her coincided with the death of Capel. According to Justine Picardie in her book *Coco Chanel: The Legend and the Life* (HarperCollins, 2010), Chanel remarked about Misia that "I have seen her appear at the moment of my greatest grieving; other people's grief lures her, just as fragrances lure the bee."

Competitiveness characterized the women's interactions although the bitterness seemed to come more from Chanel than Misia; in some ways theirs was a love/hate relationship. Friction between the two lurched into view when Chanel accompanied Misia and José on their honeymoon to Italy in 1920. Misia, a pianist, was a great patron of the arts. Sergei Diaghilev, the director of the Ballets Russes, was a fast friend. In Venice, the two were overheard by Chanel discussing how best to raise the necessary funds to revive the ballet *Le Sacre du Printemps*.

Their closeness must have struck a jealous nerve with Chanel, for as soon as they were back in Paris, Chanel approached Diaghilev with an offer to fund the production, but only if he would not breath a word of it to anyone. She must have hoped to create a bond between them that would threaten the pre-existing bond with Misia. The ruse apparently worked. The ensuing collaboration between Chanel and Diaghilev marked her official entrance into the Parisian art scene. Two years later, in 1922, Jean Cocteau asked

Coco Chanel, by Cecil Beaton, 1937, from the Cecil Beaton Studio Archive, Sotheby's London

Portrait by Horst P. Horst, 1937 (above and right)

Chanel to design the costumes for his stage adaptation of the Greek tragedy *Antigone*; Picasso was commissioned to design the sets. In 1924, the trio once again collaborated on the Ballet Russes production of *Le Train Blue*, or *The Blue Train*.

Diaghilev was not the only one of Misia's acquaintances Chanel would choose to befriend; Pierre Reverdy would be her next conquest. Reverdy was an impoverished poet living in the Bohemian section of Paris known as Montmartre when Misia first encountered him and his work. He lived with his wife, Henriette–a seamstress–and worked primarily as a writer, self-publishing poems that his wife would bind together for him. He also edited a short-lived yet influential publication, *Nord-Sud*, with Max Jacob and Guillaume Apollinaire, the latter of which was responsible for introducing Pablo Picasso to Georges Braque.

This period following World War I marked a very important time in the evolution of all things artistic, with many writers and artists living in close quarters in the City of Light, dedicating themselves to their dreams and ideas, influencing each other, converging to create something new and exciting the world had never seen. This is the culture that Misia and Chanel rubbed elbows with daily and that Misia, in particular, dedicated herself to supporting through her salons.

When Misia discovered Reverdy, she did not hesitate to usher him into her world, inviting him to dinner parties and introducing him to her friends. As did so many budding artists of the time, Reverdy owed much of his future success to Misia, just as Chanel owed her success to Capel, Balsan, and their acquaintances. Not long after Capel's death, Misia introduced Chanel to Reverdy, perhaps in an effort to get Chanel's mind off of her lover's tragic fate or as a means to shift Reverdy's affections from her to Chanel. Reverdy–despite having a wife–had fallen head over heels for Misia; his love would remain unrequited.

Once Reverdy met Chanel, he did indeed focus his affections on her and soon was dependent on her patronage. While she devoted herself to reading his prose and

Chanel reclining on the luxurious suede divan in her apartment over the Chanel boutique at 31 rue Cambon, 1937

poetry, he created a collection of her original aphorisms, or quotes. The idea to record her sayings was partially inspired by Francois de La Rochefoucauld's 17th-century publication *Maximes*. A few examples of Chanel's "maxims" edited by Reverdy include:

"If you were born without wings, do nothing to prevent their growing."

"Luxury is a necessity that begins where necessity ends."

"True generosity means accepting ingratitude."

"To disguise oneself is charming; to have oneself disguised is sad."

In 1921 Chanel hit yet another important milestone with the creation of what has become one of, if not the most, universally well-known, classic perfumes—Chanel N°5. Chanel was introduced to the prominent French parfumier Ernest Beaux, from Grasse, a coastal town in southern France

considered to be the world capital of perfume, by her then-lover, the Grand Duke Dmitri Pavlovich. Beaux was well known to Russian royalty as their parfumier of choice. With the onset of the Bolshevik Revolution, Beaux relocated to the south of France. There he established a laboratory where he attempted to replicate a scent he had first encountered in the northern wilds of Russia, so far north the sun never set on certain days of the year. The scent recalled the crystal clear arctic water of the streams, lakes, and rivers that sparkled in the ever-present sunlight and produced the freshest of nature's multitude of fragrances.

Beaux's quest captivated Chanel, no doubt not only for its grand aspirations, but also as a potential moneymaking opportunity. Beaux selected 10 variations of the scent, N°1–5 and N°20–24, from which she chose N°5. They decided to keep N°5 as the name because Chanel was presenting her new collection on the fifth day of the fifth month of the year, May 5. She firmly believed that the number five was her lucky number, this belief having its genesis in her years at the abbey in Aubazine. An anecdote about N°5 that

Hunting with Winston Churchill, who is believed to have played a major role in her exile to Switzerland after World War II when she was suspected of being a Nazi collaborator

illustrates Chanel's indomitable flair for marketing her creations goes like this: Leaving Beaux's laboratory having settled on the final scent, they dined with friends at a very fashionable restaurant. Sitting at the table, Chanel clandestinely sprayed passing female patrons with the new N°5. Later, pre-production, she continuously

Gloria Swanson wearing a Chanel design created for the 1931 movie Tonight or Never

sprayed her boutiques in Paris, Deauville, and Biarritz and would hand out sample vials to customers in a rather ahead-of-her-time marketing campaign.

The origin of the perfume bottle's iconic design is swathed in mystery. Some say Chanel designed the bottle with its square, faceted corners after a favorite decanter of Boy Capel or one of his toiletry bottles, whereas others claim its shape is reminiscent of the outline of the Place Vendôme visible from her suite at the Ritz hotel. The bottle design on store shelves today remains unchanged from its debut in 1924, although the glass stopper has experienced several iterations. The rectangular design of the glass stopper as seen from above is believed to have taken its shape from a wall mirror in Chanel's rue Cambon apartment. The original bottle design was curved and very delicate, so delicate that it could not withstand the trials of shipping necessary for wide distribution, hence the adoption of a second, sturdier design.

But the true driving force behind the perfume's success was Pierre Wertheimer who, along with his brother

On the balcony of her suite at the Ritz

Paul, owned an extremely successful cosmetics company, Bourjois. Chanel had approached Theophile Bader, owner of the department store Galeries Lafayette in Paris, about stocking her new perfume. Bader was well aware of Chanel's cachet with Parisian women and instantly realized how quickly her perfume would fly off the shelves, much more rapidly than it could currently be produced. To remedy this problem he suggested a meeting with the Wertheimer brothers to discuss moving the perfume's production to their Bourjois factory. In addition to their business expertise, the Wertheimer family were avid art collectors and owners of racehorses, elements that clicked with Chanel.

The Wertheimers' decision to produce perfume N°5 immortalized the Wertheimer name in the world of cosmetics and fragrances. Wertheimer had supreme faith in Chanel's "nose" and knew Bader would not have suggested their involvement unless he viewed this as a lucrative business deal. Today, the family still owns a controlling interest in the privately held House of Chanel. Not only did the Wertheimers produce perfume

for Chanel, they helped her create and expand a cosmetics empire that, like all of her creations, has proven to have a life of its own. A visitor to Paris can visit the House of Chanel factory, which displays the Chanel products produced there over the years.

Gloria Swanson wearing a Chanel design created for the 1931 movie Tonight or Never

Both the novelist Colette and the fashion editor Diana Vreeland described Chanel as looking like a little bull. In this photograph of Chanel, with her flaring nostrils and dark piercing eyes, it is easy to see what they meant.

In return for 10% of the profits, Chanel licensed her name as Parfums Chanel and stepped away from the daily business enterprise. The Wertheimers' agreement with Bader gave him a 20% share of the profits, so that the Wertheimer brothers benefitted from the remaining 70%, but also accepted all risk of producing and marketing the brand.

To have accepted such a small share of the profits, Chanel, as the savvy business woman she was, must have assumed the revenue from N°5 (or cosmetics, in general) would never be as profitable as it proved to be. By the World War II years, the revenue she was forgoing was evident, and she undertook to get it back. Because the Wertheimers were Jewish, to avoid Nazi persecution they fled France for the United States in 1941. As an Aryan, Chanel was able to file a petition with the German occupiers to legalize her sole ownership of the assets of Parfums Chanel. Unbeknownst to Chanel, the prescient Wertheimers had transferred legal control of the business to a Christian businessman, Felix Amiot, who ran the company during the war. Chanel was unable to secure the business's assets, and at war's end the business was returned to the Wertheimers.

In 1923, Chanel began a seven-year affair with the 44-year-old Hugh Richard Arthur Grosvenor, 2nd Duke of Westminster, the richest man in England at the time. The two met at a party in Monte Carlo after being introduced by a mutual friend, Vera Bate, connected in a rather minor way to British aristocracy. Grosvenor had lost his father as a young child. Thus, at his grandfather's death in 1899 he inherited the entire family fortune at the young age of 20.

Growing up he enjoyed a rather bohemian life filled with the love and affection of his mother, her much younger husband (only 16 years his stepson's senior), and two older sisters. As a result, Grosvenor was a very agreeable, kind, and empathetic man, who enjoyed and appreciated women, a real drawing card for the wounded Chanel. Grosvenor was married to his second wife, Violet Nelson, when he met Chanel. His first marriage to Constance Edwina Lewes had begun to disintegrate after the death from appendicitis of their only male child. The

A 1937 photo by Franz Kollar; note the sketches posted on her beloved coromandel screens of which she would eventually own 32.

duke's marriage to Violet produced no children.

Yet again, Chanel's attraction to fabulously wealthy and elite men paid off, as she was on the receiving end of a London house as well as a plot of land on the French Riviera where she would build her villa, La Pausa, whose design was inspired by the convent that sheltered her as an adolescent. The couple spent many extended vacations together at the duke's homes in England and Scotland where the couple engaged in salmon fishing, horseback riding, and playing cards by the fireplace in the evenings.

Another popular choice for getaways together was on board Grosvenor's yacht and surrogate baby, *Flying Cloud*, typically docked on the French Riviera. At the time of their meeting, Chanel was still involved with Dmitri Pavlovich, yet was growing increasingly tired of his philandering ways, a sticking point after years of hurt from Capel's romantic disloyalty. With Grosvenor, she certainly had the same concerns—he too was a well-known playboy—but his wealth and connections were staggeringly compelling. Chanel eventually succumbed to the duke, ending her relationship with Pavlovich in 1924. Grosvenor proved to be a truly beneficial alliance as she quickly found herself mingling with the best-of-the-best upper-class English set, including Winston Churchill, who took a great liking to her and would endear himself to her after World War II as she strove to protect herself from accusations that she was a Nazi collaborator.

A growing affinity for the English encouraged Chanel to take her fashions "across the pond" where they were greeted by an adoring clientele of wealthy British women. *Vogue* wrote: "Chanel, one of the most popular of great French couturiers, has come to London.... In a beautiful Queen Anne house, with paneled walls and parquet floors, mannequins graceful and slender as lilies show us Chanel's latest collection...." Chanel opened her boutique in the house Grosvenor had purchased for her, and by doing so created much speculation that they were soon to be married. The marriage never came to pass. Chanel's proclamation "there have been many Duchesses of Westminster, but only one Coco Chanel!"

Another photograph by Franz Kollar, 1937, capturing Chanel at work

Leaving the store he patted his pocket, telling Loelia, "Not for you." The marriage began as it was to end, with much unhappiness.

As Chanel's affair with Grosvenor was ending, her affair with Hollywood was just beginning. Having earned a worldwide reputation by this time, the Hollywood mogul Samuel Goldwyn approached Chanel, offering her a $1 million contract to provide her services to the Hollywood film industry. The *New York Times* reported that her services would include reorganizing the dressmaking department of the United Artists studios and anticipating fashions six months ahead, solving the studio's ongoing problem of keeping film fashions up to date.

may explain why. In 1930, having divorced Violet Nelson, the duke married an English aristocrat, Loelia Ponsonby, and his affair with Chanel came to an end. Loelia, the Duchess of Westminster, recalls in her memoir *Grace and Favour* (Reynal, 1961) being presented by the duke to Chanel in the winter of 1930 as if "for inspection." On the way to meet Chanel, Grosvenor stopped at the jeweler Van Cleef & Arpels to pick up a bauble.

Chanel's acceptance of Goldwyn's offer may have been influenced by the Great Depression. Just like every other market, the Parisian couture market was under severe stress, and she had been forced to halve her prices. The Great Depression was similarly likely a factor in Goldwyn's desire to hire Chanel. From Goldwyn's standpoint, he believed that financially

*So Chanel...draped with strands and strands of pearls and a
cigarette dangling from her fingertips*

strained American audiences would be drawn to movies filled with the alluring and glamorous fashions of Paris couture.

Misia accompanied Chanel to Hollywood and the two departed France in late February 1931. When they arrived in New York City, they boarded a train car fully decked out by Goldwyn. It was entirely white, loaded to the gills with French champagne and with reporters from every important newspaper. Arriving at Union Station in Los Angeles after their cross-country trip, the queen of fashion was greeted by none other than Greta Garbo. Despite all the fan-fare and attention, Chanel only worked on three films.

The first, *Palmy Days*, went relatively unnoticed by film critics. The deadline for the film gave Chanel scarcely enough time to do her job. One notable aspect of the film is that Chanel created a series of dresses for the leading lady, Barbara Weeks, and despite all appearing to be identical, each was slightly different. This is yet another example of Chanel's supreme attention to detail. Her goal was to complement the actress in her different scenes, using slightly different cuts and draping so that the dress would make the actress look her best on screen as the angle of the shot and the action changed.

The second film, *Tonight or Never*, starred Gloria Swanson. A year later, for the last film she worked on—*The Greeks Had a Word for Them*, also known as *Three Broadway Girls*, with Ina Claire, Joan Blondell, and Madge Evans—Chanel designed 30 dresses, most of which were finished in her Paris studio and shipped to Hollywood. Surprisingly, Goldwyn and his studio heads were disappointed with Chanel's designs, asserting that her designs were not "sensational enough" for the movies. Chanel left aggravated with the American movie scene, vowing never to work again in the States, especially Hollywood, because it was "vulgar."

Chanel's next great venture was in the world of jewelry. The International Guild of Diamond Merchants commissioned her to design a diamond jewelry collection, Bijoux de Diamants. The collection when completed was on display to the public for an admission price of 20 francs. Two days after the opening, the share price of the diamond mining company De Beers rocketed up on the London stock

Photographed at work by Roger Schall, 1937

exchange, proving that Chanel's touch was magic indeed. For herself, Chanel always claimed to prefer costume jewelry to the real thing, but the contrast between her simple yet chic clothing designs and her new opulent diamond jewelry collection complemented each other well.

Some of the most controversial and mysterious years of Chanel's life are those of World War II, when her actions, as well as her alleged anti-Semitic feelings, caused many to speculate that she was a Nazi spy and sympathizer. Throughout her life, Chanel affiliated herself with the socially and economically powerful as a means of financial self-preservation and independence. Why would her *modus operandi* change because of war? Her beloved Paris, the only real home she had ever known, had been invaded by the German army who exerted the all-encompassing power of an occupying force. Her business was no longer viable in the midst of war. The astute Chanel certainly knew on which side her bread was buttered and acted accordingly.

The fact that Chanel stayed in Paris and rubbed elbows with the Nazi occupiers is obviously damaging to her claim of French and Allied patriotism when so many people did flee and lost so much in an effort to remove themselves, their families, and businesses from the taint of National Socialism. The truth of the matter will likely never be known, whether because no valid support exists for such claims of collaboration or because her connections to the Duke of Westminster and Churchill, among others, allowed such support to be swept under the rug.

Her Allied allegiance was questioned largely because of her affair with the German aristocrat Baron Hans Günther von Dincklage, known to his friends as Spatz. Born to a British mother and German father, Spatz had been in Paris since 1928. His marriage to a half-Jewish German woman, whom he divorced in 1935, did nothing to deter his rather rakish tendencies in the racy milieu of pre-war Paris. Chanel claims to have known him or known of him during these years, but did not begin her affair with him until 1941. In his controversial book *Sleeping with the Enemy: Coco Chanel's Secret War* (Knopf/Random House, 2011), Hal Vaughan, a U.S. veteran, journalist, and diplomat who retired

1952

in Paris, provides what he views as a plethora of documentation from recently declassified government documents that unquestionably proves von Dincklage was an Abwehr (German military intelligence) spy as well as Chanel.

In 1939, as the war started in full force, Chanel shut her boutiques, leaving her Paris shop open only for the sale of perfumes and accessories. In 1940, she launched a new fragrance, Biege de Chanel. Others, such as Elsa Schiaparelli, a major rival, as well as Molyneux and Lanvin, vowed to keep their couture businesses going as much to provide needed jobs in war-torn France as an attempt to maintain the status quo in the face of the unimaginable turn of events.

A line of reality was drawn, however, when in May 1940 German troops encroached on Paris. All couture businesses were shuttered. Chanel packed her belongings in various trunks, stored them at the Ritz, paid her bill two months in advance, and departed Paris in her (now drafted) chauffer's personal car instead of her black Rolls-Royce, which she was advised would stand out like a sore thumb.

Traveling with Chanel were several of her female employees who had been working with her since her earliest days as a milliner. They traveled to the Pyrenees where Chanel had bought a house many years before for her nephew, André Palasse, who had by then left to join the French army. André would eventually be captured by the Germans and sent to a prisoner-of-war camp, one of the events that set in motion Chanel's deeper involvement with the Germans.

André's daughter, Chanel's namesake Gabrielle, was at the house, and as Justine Picardie tells it in her biography of Chanel, remembers their arrival in this way: "She came in the car with her maid, and a few other women–one of them was Madame Aubert–so it was quite a job finding places for all of them to stay. Auntie Coco had somehow managed to send on her entire gold dressing table set which had been given to her by my godfather, the Duke of Westminster, and that came to our house separately.... She was already staying with us by the time the Armistice was signed [on June 22, 1940]–we listened to the news on the radio, and she wept bitterly." France had surrendered to Hitler.

The designer at work, photographed for Vogue *magazine
by Henry Clarke, 1954*

Chanel and her entourage remained at the Pyrenees house for the summer, naturally afraid to return to Paris and of what they would find there if they did. At some point, her friend Marie-Louise Bousquet arrived at the Pyrenees house and the two conceived a plan to make their way back to Paris. After the expected detours and delays, the two completed the journey. Chanel naturally gravitated to the Ritz, filled to the rafters with German officers. As was Chanel's way, she persuaded the Germans to let her stay at the hotel, and the hotel's management found her a small room.

Even though she didn't begin her affair with the much younger von Dincklage until 1941, Chanel had been under suspicion by the French police since 1929. Her good friend Vera Bate, who had introduced her to the Duke of Westminster in 1923, had married Colonel Alberto Lombardi. Both were suspected German spies.

When she learned of her nephew's capture by the Germans, Chanel implored von Dincklage to help her negotiate André's release from the German POW camp, but his attempts at doing so were not successful. Next, Chanel turned to Spatz's friend Captain Theodore Momm, but he also was unable to achieve André's release. During the ensuing negotiations in the fall of 1943, the Nazi chief of foreign intelligence, Walter Shellenburg, approached Chanel about carrying a clandestine letter to the British, aware of her close association with Churchill, to alert the Allies that certain senior German commanders were no longer supportive of Hitler. The mission was named Operation Modellhut (Model Hat).

From here the plot is murky to say the least. The plan was either for Chanel or her friend Vera Lombardi (or both) to deliver the letter to the British ambassador, Sir Samuel Hoare, in Madrid. Accounts of the story from the major players differ. Chanel may or may not have traveled to Madrid and/or Berlin. Her possible trip to Madrid may or may not have been with Vera, who had been arrested in Italy and was being held as a British spy, but was subsequently released due to German intervention to make the trip to Madrid. Vera did by all accounts arrive in Madrid and immediately gave up Chanel—true or not—as a German spy. Schellenberg promptly dropped all contact

Photographed by Willy Rizzo at the Tuilleries gardens in Paris, 1957

with Lombardi and Chanel, not desiring to draw unwanted attention to himself and his compatriots who were attempting communication that would have been a death sentence had Hitler known.

In September 1944, Chanel was questioned by the French authorities about her involvement with the Nazis during the war, but that brief encounter was basically the end of the inquiry with the exception of an appearance in 1949 at the war crimes trial of Baron Louis de Vaufreland, a German intelligence officer. Speculation remains that Churchill intervened not only to save his friend Chanel, but also to save many members of the British aristocracy from being implicated as Nazi sympathizers should Chanel have to spill all.

Chanel left Paris in 1945, moving to Switzerland where she would remain until 1954 when she once again returned to Paris to revive her fashion empire. During her early days in Switzerland, she enlisted her good friend and writer Paul Morand to immortalize her life's story. The two met in a St. Moritz hotel in 1946 where she freely offered her opinions, philosophies, and tales of the rich and

famous, including Misia Sert, Serge Lifar, Jean Cocteau, Pablo Picasso, and Winston Churchill. The result was a small volume, presented as a conversation between the two, called *The Allure of Chanel*. Morand's book was recently updated with 73 sketches by Karl Lagerfield, the head designer and creative director of Chanel since the early 1980s, published in the U.S. and U.K. in 2013 by Pushkin.

Chanel left retirement at the age of 70 to combat what she viewed as the re-emergence of constrictive couture, primarily emanating from the drawing boards of Christian Dior. For so many

Leaving Dallas with Neiman Marcus hatbox in hand as Stanley Marcus bids her "adieu," 1957

*With Stanley Marcus of Neiman Marcus department
stores on a visit to Dallas, 1957*

*At work (above);
a fitting with
the model Paule
Rizzo, 1950s
(right)*

A needed adjustment, 1950s

years she had struggled to overcome fashionable clothing that did not allow women to be and feel free, and she just could not ignore the direction the fashion industry was taking—a U turn. The critics, particularly those in Europe, were rather vicious toward her return. But Bettina Ballard, fashion editor of *Vogue*, remained true to Chanel and positively reviewed her collection, proclaiming it classic. Ballard had a wicked pen. Before the war she was in Paris as *Vogue's* American representative. She relayed daily dispatches to the staff. In one she recounted watching an unrepentant Chanel steer her dance partner as well as her rival, Elsa Schiaperelli, dressed as a Surrealist tree, into a standing candelabra at the Bal de la Forêt. Schiaperelli, in flames, was quickly doused with soda water by nearby guests.

With a negative reception in Europe, Chanel focused her sights on America. *Life* magazine helped her gain traction in the States with a four-page spread published in 1954 titled "The Name behind the Most Famous Perfume in the

Surrounded by the models Ghislaine Arsac, Marie-Hélène Arnaud, Suzy Parker, Odile de Cröy, Paule Rizzo, Mimi d'Arcangues, Gisèle Rosenthal and Paule de Mérindol in 1959

Reviewing her handiwork as a model poses, 1958

World." The magazine ignored the rumors surrounding Chanel during the war years and loudly applauded her latest designs. To everyone's surprise (and Ballard's vindication), Chanel's new collection was an uncompromising hit and her workshop was flooded with orders, not only from America but also from Europe. Chanel's designs remained timeless, as well as practical, rising to the demands of the modern woman. Celebrities, royals, the fashion elite, everyone recognized this incontrovertible truth no matter their opinions of her past. The proof was self-evident. Chanel's design acumen was a force to be reckoned with.

To celebrate her rise from the ashes of retirement and tainted reputation, Chanel reintroduced her classic handbag in 1955. She named the quilted, gold-chain-wrapped strapped bag 2.55 after the month she created it, February 1955. It is doubtful that the appearance of two fives, Chanel's lucky number, is merely coincidence.

In 1957, on the occasion of the 50th anniversary of the Texas-headquartered Neiman Marcus luxury department store, Chanel received an award from its president, Stanley Marcus, proclaiming her "the most influential designer of the twentieth century." Chanel flew to Dallas, Texas, for the award ceremony. After a three-week stay she jetted to New York City to be interviewed by *New Yorker* magazine. It's no wonder that after the aloofness and criticism of the Europeans (justified or not), Chanel was thrilled to be in the welcoming, relaxed, and accepting United States.

When Chanel returned to Paris in 1954 to reopen her couture salon, she sold her beloved villa, La Pausa, on the French Riviera to an American couple from Texas, Emery Reves and his wife, Wendy. After living in the villa for almost 30 years, Reves' widow donated much of the furniture and artwork in the villa to the Dallas Museum of Art, where five rooms of La Pausa have been recreated and are on display.

For years, Chanel followed a sacred routine. As she left the Ritz, where she slept night after night, for the five-minute walk to 31 rue Cambon, the hotel called ahead to say she was on her way. The

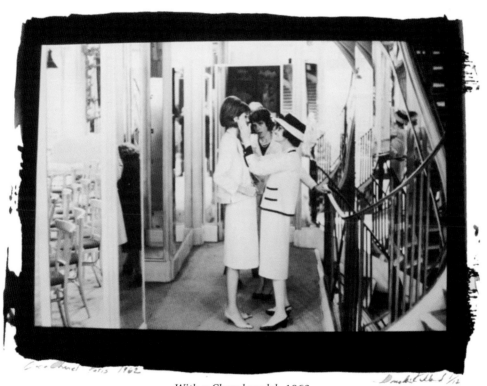

With a Chanel model, 1962

call signaled a liberal spraying of her signature scent, Chanel N°5, along the staircase that rose to her rue Cambon apartment. The moment Chanel entered her boutique an assistant gracefully draped a pair of scissors attached to a long white ribbon around the designer's neck. No doubt Chanel chose a white ribbon to blend easily with the multiple strands of white pearls she always wore around her neck; every special occasion had been justification for yet another strand, happily bestowed on her by the Duke of Westminster throughout their seven years together.

Throughout her life, Chanel strove for perfection, known to alter one suit in the minutest ways up to 35 times in a sitting. As she aged, Chanel focused on her true love: innovative, but practical fashion. She worked until she could work no longer. Death claimed her suddenly. Working feverishly on a Saturday to complete her new collection, she was forced to relax the following day because it was Sunday. After a leisurely lunch with her dear friend Claude Delay at the Ritz, they went for a drive through the streets of Paris, observing the crowds from a safely removed distance. When she returned after dark to the Ritz, she lay down on the bed fully clothed, too exhausted to ask her maid Céline for help to undress. It wasn't long before Chanel called out to Céline that she was having difficulty breathing. Céline went to her mistress after opening a window and attempted to help Chanel inject herself in the hip with her nightly dose of morphine, taken for many years to help her sleep. In the morning, Chanel's soul was gone.

At the age of 87, Chanel was buried wearing one of her white suits, her casket dressed in white flowers—camellias, gardenias, orchids, and azaleas—and a single wreath of red roses. The funeral service was at L'Eglise de la Madeleine, a church not far from rue Cambon. She was buried in Lausanne, Switzerland, on the banks of Lac Leman. Chanel's funeral was attended by her models, dressed like little soldiers in their leader's designs. The other prominent couturiers—Balmain, Balenciaga, Courrèges—also paid their respects to the indomitable Coco. So many of Chanel's partners in crime had preceded her in death, but Salvadore Dalí, with whom she was rumored to have had an affair, was there to say one last and heartfelt good-bye.

COCO CHANEL: HER PERFUMES

The drawing above, by the artist Sem, was the original advertisement for Chanel N°5 perfume. The ad on the opposite page first ran in 1937. Chanel represented her own scent, posed leaning on the mantle of the fireplace in her apartment at the Ritz hotel in Paris. The text reads: "Madame Gabrielle Chanel is above all an artist in living. Her dresses, her perfumes, are created with a faultless instinct for drama. Her Perfume N°5 is like the soft music that underlies the playing of a love scene. It kindles the imagination; indelibly fixes the scene in the memories of the players." The other Chanel perfumes at the time were Glamour de Chanel, Gardenia de Chanel, and Cuir de Russe (Russian Leather). Today's collection includes Chanel's namesake fragrance Coco and its variations—Coco Mademoiselle and Coco Noir—Chance, N°19 (her birthdate), Allure, and Cristalle.

Madame Gabrielle Chanel in her new apartment in the Ritz, Paris

Photo by Kollar, courtesy Harper's Bazaar

Madame Gabrielle Chanel is above all an artist in living. Her dresses, her perfumes, are created with a faultless instinct for drama. Her Perfume No. 5 is like the soft music that underlies the playing of a love scene. It kindles the imagination; indelibly fixes the scene in the memories of the players.

LES PARFUMS

CHANEL

GLAMOUR de CHANEL   GARDENIA de CHANEL   CUIR de RUSSIE (Russia Leather)

COCO CHANEL: HER CLOTHES

C hanel is almost completely single-handedly responsible for the way women
dress today. The number of firsts that she racked up is unprecedented.
It all began with a simple decoration aptly placed on a straw boater, then
unconstructed sweaters of wool jersey, the chemise dress, ankle-baring skirts
topped by belted coats, and wide sailor-collared blouses with large pockets
intended to be used. During World War I she trimmed her coats in fur, using
beaver and rabbit which were much easier to come by than finer furs (and were
also more affordable) and introduced lounging pajamas, cardigans, and twinsets.
She matched coat linings with blouses. After the war, in tribute to her current
love interest, Russian Grand Duke Dmitri Pavlovich, Chanel embroidered peasant
blouses, using sophisticated fabrics such as black crepe de chine. Sporting wide-
bottomed trousers and cork-soled sandals on the Lido in Venice, she began yet
another trend. She used square necklines when other fashion houses were not,
and draped her models in strand after strand of faux pearls, reminiscent of her
pearls, gifts from the Duke of Westminster. It was Chanel who first strove to
design costume jewelry that looked real (*vrais bijoux en toc*). During her lengthy
relationship with the Duke of Westminster, she brought tweed into her collection.
She dropped waistlines, raised hemlines further, and fashioned the first "little
black dress," a straight-lined little number in the *garçonne*, or "little boy,"
style. In 1929, inspired by soldiers' satchels, Chanel added straps to handbags
so women could carry them easily on their shoulders. After her return to the
fashion industry in 1954, Chanel updated her classic strapped bag, naming it 2.55
in honor of its creation in February 1955, and reintroduced two-tone pumps.
Chanel shirked the mini-skirt, relying instead on the classic suits and accessories
she believed best flattered the female form. *Vogue* magazine quotes the grand
couturier as calling short skirts "the most absurd weapon woman has ever
employed to seduce men."

Prêt-á-porter (ready-to-wear) casual jersey dresses, 1917

COCO CHANEL: HER CLOTHES

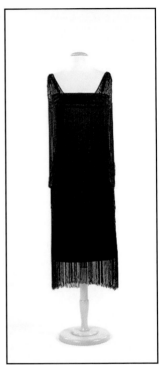

Chanel's "little black dress" first introduced in 1926 as seen in a fashion magazine of the era (left) and in the collection of the Metropolitan Museum of Art, New York City, dating from 1924-25 (above)

In 1924, Chanel designed costumes for the Ballet Russes production The Blue Train. *The costumes are now housed at the Victoria and Albert Museum in London. The two shown above were created from knitted wool and wool, respectively.*

COCO CHANEL: HER CLOTHES

A black cocktail dress, c. 1957, in the collection of the Metropolitan Museum of Art, New York City (left); the classic 2.55 quilted flap bag named after the date it was created, February 1955 (below). Chanel introduced its predecessor in 1929, but updated the design to celebrate her comeback in the fashion industry a year earlier. A sketch for one design of many of the Chanel suit from the 1950s-60s (right).

CHANEL
B 60

81

COCO CHANEL: HER QUOTES

"As long as you know men are like children, you know everything!"

"In order to be irreplaceable one must always be different."

"A girl should be two things: classy and fabulous."

"Fashion is not something that exists in dresses only. Fashion is in the sky, in the street, fashion has to do with ideas, the way we live, what is happening."

"A women who doesn't wear perfume has no future."

"Fashion fades, only style remains the same."

"Elegance is not the prerogative of those who have just escaped from adolescence, but of those who have already taken possession of their future."

"Some people think luxury is the opposite of poverty. It is not. It is the opposite of vulgarity."

"Fashion is architecture: it is a matter of proportions."

"Elegance does not consist in putting on a new dress."

A portrait by Boris Lipnitski, 1936

COCO CHANEL: HER QUOTES

"Luxury must be comfortable, otherwise it is not luxury."

"Fashion is made to become unfashionable."

"I am against fashion that doesn't last. I cannot accept that you throw your clothes away just because it is spring."

"It is always better to be slightly underdressed."

"There have been several Duchesses of Westminster but there is only one Chanel!"

"Simplicity is the keynote of all true elegance."

"Nature gives you the face you have at twenty. Life shapes the face you have at thirty. But at fifty you get the face you deserve."

"Elegance comes from being as beautiful inside as outside."

"Nothing is more beautiful than freedom of the body."

"Look for the woman in the dress. If there is no woman, there is no dress."

COCO CHANEL: HER APARTMENT

C hanel never slept in her apartment over her boutique, preferring instead to sleep at the Ritz, a short walk away. She filled her rue Cambon apartment with all the things she loved: coromandel screens, vermeille cigarette boxes given to her by the Duke of Westminster, tailored furniture, crystal balls, books, repeated motifs of shafts of wheat, lions to celebrate her birth sign of Leo, and her lucky number five, found even in the gilded arms of a chandeleir.

Chanel covered her deep sofa in beige suede, an unusual fabric choice for the era. As always, she anticipated the future of design, be it in clothing or in interiors.

COCO CHANEL: HER APARTMENT

Chanel's apartment remains as it was on the day she died in 1971, an avowal of her elegant taste, her love of luxury— with the exception of two items. The silk slipper chair on which she was reclining when photographed by Horst in 1937 (right) was purchased at auction and added to the apartment's furnishings as well as a small chair that Chanel sat in to do her fittings. The energy of Chanel that reverberates in her apartment is only intensified by these two very personal furnishings.

Chanel standing in the salon of her 31 rue Cambon apartment (opposite page); a modern facsimile of the gilt sheaf-of-wheat table base that appears to her immediate left in the photograph is shown at right with a glass top. Chanel in her inimitable way had topped it with a laquered black tray with inlaid design.

COCO CHANEL: HER CLIENTS

Immediately popular with the artistocratic and wealthy set, Chanel's fashions have always adorned high-profile clients who very effectively marketed her clothes, hats, and accessories for her—simply through the act of wearing them. In the 1920s, her clients expanded to the dancers of the Ballet Russes and the actors in her friend Jean Cocteau's plays, and in the 1930s to movie stars after a short-lived stint in Hollywood under a $1 million contract to Samuel Goldwyn's United Artists studio. Both Greta Garbo and Marlene Dietrich became big fans of Chanel.

After her return from exile in Switzerland in 1954, Chanel was asked to costume several actresses in French films, among them Ingrid Bergman, Jeanne Moreau, and Delphine Seyrig. Grace Kelly, Rita Hayworth, Elizabeth Taylor, Romy Schneider, Barbra Streisand, and Jackie Kennedy were just a few of the highly photographed women who wore Chanel's designs for the world to see. And Marilyn Monroe quipped that the only thing she wore to bed was a few drops of Chanel

N°5. Since Chanel's death in 1971, the fashion empire the designer, innovator, and style-setter built and rebuilt continues to thrive, dressing the likes of Princess Diana, Madonna, and Jerry Hall.

Grace Kelly, Princess of Monaco, in a tweed suit by Chanel

Marilyn Monroe applying Chanel N°5, 1954

COCO CHANEL: HER CLIENTS

Elizabeth Taylor, accompanied by her husband Eddie Fisher, wears Chanel, 1961.

Chanel outfitted Jeanne Moreau for Roger Vadim's Les Liaisons Dangereuses; *Moreau is wearing a Chanel suit on a visit with the designer in her rue Cambon apartment, 1959.*

It is now believed that the iconic pink suit Jackie Kennedy wore on November 22, 1963, in Dallas was a Chanel knock-off made in New York City's Garment District.

COCO CHANEL: HER RIVAL

P aul Poiret, who introduced the kimono coat in the early 1900s, paved the way for the unstructured, uncorseted clothes championed by Chanel and her main rival in the years between the two world wars, the Italian-born Elsa Schiaperelli. Schiaperelli's designs were hugely influenced by Surrealist artists, such as Salvador Dalí and Alberto Giacometti, who were her friends. Just like Poiret, for whom World War I marked the end of a thriving business, World War II began the decline of Schiaperelli's fashion house. Schiaperelli was unable to adjust to the post-war design aesthetic and closed her business in 1954, the same year Chanel reappeared in Paris to reclaim her reputation.

A model posing in a Schiaparelli suit outside the designer's Place Vendôme shop, 1947 (left), Schiaperelli wearing an evening dress of her own design, 1929 (immediate right), and in a moment of repose (far right)